V - COUNTRY VOTING PRACTICES

This section consolidates previous information, and presents it by country for 190 UN members (all except the United States). The countries appear in alphabetical order as they are seated at the UN General Assembly. Thus, the Democratic People's Republic of Korea is listed under "D," Republic of Korea and Republic of Moldova under "R," The Former Yugoslav Republic of Macedonia under "T," and United Republic of Tanzania under "U." The Democratic Republic of the Congo, formerly Zaire, is listed under "D." Congo (Brazzaville) remains at "C". Burma, which changed its name to Myanmar and is so designated at the United Nations, is listed under "M." Ivory Coast, which changed its name to Cote d'Ivoire, appears under "C." Each country listing contains the following:

— Summary coincidence percentages drawn from Sections III and IV, and, for Security Council members, Section II. Coincidence percentages for selected issue categories are included; they are derived by the same methodology used for overall Plenary votes, i.e., identical votes divided by the sum of identical and opposite votes; abstentions and absences are not included, nor are consensus resolutions.

— Vote totals in the Plenary and on the 14 important Plenary votes.

— Every vote on the 14 important issues, with the U.S. vote in parentheses for comparison. Symbols used are Y=Yes, N=No, A=Abstain, and X=Absent.

Countries two years in arrears in payment of UN dues are not permitted to vote in the Plenary. For 2002, these countries included: the Central African Republic, Iraq, Liberia, and Niger. Neither Palestine nor the Palestine Liberation Organization has voting privileges at the United Nations.

AFGHANISTAN

Voting Coincidence Percentages

<u>Overall Votes (90)</u>: Agree 9, Disagree 33, Abstain 0, Absent 48: 21.4%
— Including All 234 Consensus Resolutions: 79.2%
— Arms Control: 31.6%; Human Rights: 14.3%; Middle East: 0.0%

<u>Important Votes (14)</u>: Agree 1, Disagree 7, Abstain 0, Absent 6: 12.5%
— Including the 18 Important Consensus Resolutions: 58.8%

Important Issues   VOTES

1.	IAEA Report	(Y)	X
2.	U.S. Embargo of Cuba	(N)	Y
3.	National Legislation on Transfer of Arms	(Y)	Y
4.	Nuclear Disarmament	(N)	Y
5.	Risk of Nuclear Proliferation in the Middle East	(N)	Y
6.	Work of the Special Committee to Investigate Israeli Practices	(N)	X
7.	Future Operations of INSTRAW	(N)	Y
8.	Rights of the Child	(N)	Y
9.	Elimination of Racism and Racial Discrimination	(N)	Y
10.	Optional Protocol to the Convention Against Torture	(N)	X
11.	Globalization and Human Rights	(N)	Y
12.	Human Rights in Sudan	(Y)	X
13.	Human Rights in Iraq	(Y)	X
14.	Human Rights in the Congo	(Y)	X

ALBANIA

Voting Coincidence Percentages

<u>Overall Votes (90)</u>: Agree 31, Disagree 33, Abstain 16, Absent 10: 48.4%
— Including All 234 Consensus Resolutions: 87.8%
— Arms Control: 63.2%; Human Rights: 58.6%; Middle East: 33.3%

<u>Important Votes (14)</u>: Agree 5, Disagree 6, Abstain 2, Absent 1: 45.5%
— Including the 18 Important Consensus Resolutions: 77.7%

Important Issues   VOTES

1.	IAEA Report	(Y)	X
2.	U.S. Embargo of Cuba	(N)	Y
3.	National Legislation on Transfer of Arms	(Y)	Y
4.	Nuclear Disarmament	(N)	Y
5.	Risk of Nuclear Proliferation in the Middle East	(N)	Y
6.	Work of the Special Committee to Investigate Israeli Practices	(N)	A
7.	Future Operations of INSTRAW	(N)	A
8.	Rights of the Child	(N)	Y
9.	Elimination of Racism and Racial Discrimination	(N)	Y
10.	Optional Protocol to the Convention Against Torture	(N)	Y
11.	Globalization and Human Rights	(N)	N
12.	Human Rights in Sudan	(Y)	Y
13.	Human Rights in Iraq	(Y)	Y
14.	Human Rights in the Congo	(Y)	Y

Votes: Y=Yes, N=No, A=Abstain, X=Absent, ( )=U.S. Vote

ALGERIA

Voting Coincidence Percentages

Overall Votes (90): Agree 9, Disagree 61, Abstain 18, Absent 2: 12.9%
— Including All 234 Consensus Resolutions: 79.5%
— Arms Control: 20.0%; Human Rights: 5.3%; Middle East: 17.4%

Important Votes (14): Agree 2, Disagree 9, Abstain 3, Absent 0: 18.2%
— Including the 18 Important Consensus Resolutions: 68.4%

Important Issues	VOTES	
1. IAEA Report	(Y)	Y
2. U.S. Embargo of Cuba	(N)	Y
3. National Legislation on Transfer of Arms	(Y)	Y
4. Nuclear Disarmament	(N)	Y
5. Risk of Nuclear Proliferation in the Middle East	(N)	Y
6. Work of the Special Committee to Investigate Israeli Practices	(N)	Y
7. Future Operations of INSTRAW	(N)	Y
8. Rights of the Child	(N)	Y
9. Elimination of Racism and Racial Discrimination	(N)	Y
10. Optional Protocol to the Convention Against Torture	(N)	A
11. Globalization and Human Rights	(N)	Y
12. Human Rights in Sudan	(Y)	N
13. Human Rights in Iraq	(Y)	A
14. Human Rights in the Congo	(Y)	A

ANDORRA

Voting Coincidence Percentages

Overall Votes (90): Agree 37, Disagree 42, Abstain 11, Absent 0: 46.8%
— Including All 234 Consensus Resolutions: 86.6%
— Arms Control: 63.0%; Human Rights: 58.6%; Middle East: 44.0%

Important Votes (14): Agree 6, Disagree 7, Abstain 1, Absent 0: 46.2%
— Including the 18 Important Consensus Resolutions: 77.4%

Important Issues	VOTES	
1. IAEA Report	(Y)	Y
2. U.S. Embargo of Cuba	(N)	Y
3. National Legislation on Transfer of Arms	(Y)	Y
4. Nuclear Disarmament	(N)	Y
5. Risk of Nuclear Proliferation in the Middle East	(N)	Y
6. Work of the Special Committee to Investigate Israeli Practices	(N)	A
7. Future Operations of INSTRAW	(N)	Y
8. Rights of the Child	(N)	Y
9. Elimination of Racism and Racial Discrimination	(N)	Y
10. Optional Protocol to the Convention Against Torture	(N)	Y
11. Globalization and Human Rights	(N)	N
12. Human Rights in Sudan	(Y)	Y
13. Human Rights in Iraq	(Y)	Y
14. Human Rights in the Congo	(Y)	Y

Votes: Y=Yes, N=No, A=Abstain, X=Absent, ( )=U.S. Vote

3

ANGOLA

Voting Coincidence Percentages

<u>Overall Votes (90):</u> Agree 12, Disagree 57, Abstain 10, Absent 11: 17.4%
— Including All 234 Consensus Resolutions: 79.5%
— Arms Control: 25.0%; Human Rights: 16.7%; Middle East: 8.3%

<u>Important Votes (14):</u> Agree 1, Disagree 9, Abstain 4, Absent 0: 10.0%
— Including the 18 Important Consensus Resolutions: 65.6%

Important Issues   VOTES

1.	IAEA Report	(Y)	A
2.	U.S. Embargo of Cuba	(N)	Y
3.	National Legislation on Transfer of Arms	(Y)	Y
4.	Nuclear Disarmament	(N)	Y
5.	Risk of Nuclear Proliferation in the Middle East	(N)	Y
6.	Work of the Special Committee to Investigate Israeli Practices	(N)	Y
7.	Future Operations of INSTRAW	(N)	Y
8.	Rights of the Child	(N)	Y
9.	Elimination of Racism and Racial Discrimination	(N)	Y
10.	Optional Protocol to the Convention Against Torture	(N)	Y
11.	Globalization and Human Rights	(N)	Y
12.	Human Rights in Sudan	(Y)	A
13.	Human Rights in Iraq	(Y)	A
14.	Human Rights in the Congo	(Y)	A

ANTIGUA AND BARBUDA

Voting Coincidence Percentages

<u>Overall Votes (90):</u> Agree 15, Disagree 42, Abstain 2, Absent 31: 26.3%
— Including All 234 Consensus Resolutions: 79.1%
— Arms Control: 0.0%; Human Rights: 36.7%; Middle East: 27.3%

<u>Important Votes (14):</u> Agree 2, Disagree 7, Abstain 1, Absent 4: 22.2%
— Including the 18 Important Consensus Resolutions: 65.1%

Important Issues   VOTES

1.	IAEA Report	(Y)	X
2.	U.S. Embargo of Cuba	(N)	Y
3.	National Legislation on Transfer of Arms	(Y)	X
4.	Nuclear Disarmament	(N)	X
5.	Risk of Nuclear Proliferation in the Middle East	(N)	X
6.	Work of the Special Committee to Investigate Israeli Practices	(N)	Y
7.	Future Operations of INSTRAW	(N)	Y
8.	Rights of the Child	(N)	Y
9.	Elimination of Racism and Racial Discrimination	(N)	Y
10.	Optional Protocol to the Convention Against Torture	(N)	Y
11.	Globalization and Human Rights	(N)	Y
12.	Human Rights in Sudan	(Y)	A
13.	Human Rights in Iraq	(Y)	Y
14.	Human Rights in the Congo	(Y)	Y

Votes: Y=Yes, N=No, A=Abstain, X=Absent, ( )=U.S. Vote

ARGENTINA

Voting Coincidence Percentages

Overall Votes (90): Agree 26, Disagree 50, Abstain 14, Absent 0: 34.2%
— Including All 234 Consensus Resolutions: 83.9%
— Arms Control: 50.0%; Human Rights: 42.9%; Middle East: 42.3%

Important Votes (14): Agree 5, Disagree 7, Abstain 2, Absent 0: 41.7%
— Including the 18 Important Consensus Resolutions: 76.7%

Important Issues		**VOTES**
1.	IAEA Report	(Y) Y
2.	U.S. Embargo of Cuba	(N) Y
3.	National Legislation on Transfer of Arms	(Y) Y
4.	Nuclear Disarmament	(N) Y
5.	Risk of Nuclear Proliferation in the Middle East	(N) Y
6.	Work of the Special Committee to Investigate Israeli Practices	(N) A
7.	Future Operations of INSTRAW	(N) Y
8.	Rights of the Child	(N) Y
9.	Elimination of Racism and Racial Discrimination	(N) Y
10.	Optional Protocol to the Convention Against Torture	(N) Y
11.	Globalization and Human Rights	(N) A
12.	Human Rights in Sudan	(Y) Y
13.	Human Rights in Iraq	(Y) Y
14.	Human Rights in the Congo	(Y) Y

ARMENIA

Voting Coincidence Percentages

Overall Votes (90): Agree 22, Disagree 53, Abstain 14, Absent 1: 29.3%
— Including All 234 Consensus Resolutions: 82.7%
— Arms Control: 52.4%; Human Rights: 29.6%; Middle East: 29.2%

Important Votes (14): Agree 4, Disagree 8, Abstain 1, Absent 1: 33.3%
— Including the 18 Important Consensus Resolutions: 73.2%

Important Issues		**VOTES**
1.	IAEA Report	(Y) Y
2.	U.S. Embargo of Cuba	(N) Y
3.	National Legislation on Transfer of Arms	(Y) Y
4.	Nuclear Disarmament	(N) Y
5.	Risk of Nuclear Proliferation in the Middle East	(N) Y
6.	Work of the Special Committee to Investigate Israeli Practices	(N) Y
7.	Future Operations of INSTRAW	(N) Y
8.	Rights of the Child	(N) Y
9.	Elimination of Racism and Racial Discrimination	(N) Y
10.	Optional Protocol to the Convention Against Torture	(N) Y
11.	Globalization and Human Rights	(N) Y
12.	Human Rights in Sudan	(Y) X
13.	Human Rights in Iraq	(Y) Y
14.	Human Rights in the Congo	(Y) Y

Votes: Y=Yes, N=No, A=Abstain, X=Absent, ( )=U.S. Vote

AUSTRALIA

Voting Coincidence Percentages

<u>Overall Votes (90)</u>: Agree 38, Disagree 35, Abstain 17, Absent 0: 52.1%
— Including All 234 Consensus Resolutions: 88.6%
— Arms Control: 66.7%; Human Rights: 66.7%; Middle East: 44.0%

<u>Important Votes (14)</u>: Agree 7, Disagree 4, Abstain 3, Absent 0: 63.6%
— Including the 18 Important Consensus Resolutions: 86.2%

Important Issues / VOTES

1.	IAEA Report	(Y)	Y
2.	U.S. Embargo of Cuba	(N)	Y
3.	National Legislation on Transfer of Arms	(Y)	Y
4.	Nuclear Disarmament	(N)	Y
5.	Risk of Nuclear Proliferation in the Middle East	(N)	A
6.	Work of the Special Committee to Investigate Israeli Practices	(N)	A
7.	Future Operations of INSTRAW	(N)	N
8.	Rights of the Child	(N)	Y
9.	Elimination of Racism and Racial Discrimination	(N)	A
10.	Optional Protocol to the Convention Against Torture	(N)	A
11.	Globalization and Human Rights	(N)	N
12.	Human Rights in Sudan	(Y)	Y
13.	Human Rights in Iraq	(Y)	Y
14.	Human Rights in the Congo	(Y)	Y

AUSTRIA

Voting Coincidence Percentages

<u>Overall Votes (90)</u>: Agree 36, Disagree 41, Abstain 13, Absent 0: 46.8%
— Including All 234 Consensus Resolutions: 86.8%
— Arms Control: 61.5%; Human Rights: 58.6%; Middle East: 44.0%

<u>Important Votes (14)</u>: Agree 6, Disagree 6, Abstain 2, Absent 0: 50.0%
— Including the 18 Important Consensus Resolutions: 80.0%

Important Issues / VOTES

1.	IAEA Report	(Y)	Y
2.	U.S. Embargo of Cuba	(N)	Y
3.	National Legislation on Transfer of Arms	(Y)	Y
4.	Nuclear Disarmament	(N)	Y
5.	Risk of Nuclear Proliferation in the Middle East	(N)	Y
6.	Work of the Special Committee to Investigate Israeli Practices	(N)	A
7.	Future Operations of INSTRAW	(N)	A
8.	Rights of the Child	(N)	Y
9.	Elimination of Racism and Racial Discrimination	(N)	Y
10.	Optional Protocol to the Convention Against Torture	(N)	Y
11.	Globalization and Human Rights	(N)	N
12.	Human Rights in Sudan	(Y)	Y
13.	Human Rights in Iraq	(Y)	Y
14.	Human Rights in the Congo	(Y)	Y

Votes: Y=Yes, N=No, A=Abstain, X=Absent, ( )=U.S. Vote

AZERBAIJAN

Voting Coincidence Percentages

Overall Votes (90): Agree 14, Disagree 51, Abstain 22, Absent 3: 21.5%
— Including All 234 Consensus Resolutions: 82.6%
— Arms Control: 45.5%; Human Rights: 11.8%; Middle East: 21.7%

Important Votes (14): Agree 2, Disagree 10, Abstain 2, Absent 0: 16.7%
— Including the 18 Important Consensus Resolutions: 66.1%

Important Issues		**VOTES**	
1.	IAEA Report	(Y)	Y
2.	U.S. Embargo of Cuba	(N)	Y
3.	National Legislation on Transfer of Arms	(Y)	Y
4.	Nuclear Disarmament	(N)	Y
5.	Risk of Nuclear Proliferation in the Middle East	(N)	Y
6.	Work of the Special Committee to Investigate Israeli Practices	(N)	Y
7.	Future Operations of INSTRAW	(N)	Y
8.	Rights of the Child	(N)	Y
9.	Elimination of Racism and Racial Discrimination	(N)	Y
10.	Optional Protocol to the Convention Against Torture	(N)	Y
11.	Globalization and Human Rights	(N)	Y
12.	Human Rights in Sudan	(Y)	N
13.	Human Rights in Iraq	(Y)	A
14.	Human Rights in the Congo	(Y)	A

BAHAMAS

Voting Coincidence Percentages

Overall Votes (90): Agree 21, Disagree 56, Abstain 11, Absent 2: 27.3%
— Including All 234 Consensus Resolutions: 81.7%
— Arms Control: 34.5%; Human Rights: 30.4%; Middle East: 26.1%

Important Votes (14): Agree 5, Disagree 7, Abstain 2, Absent 0: 41.7%
— Including the 18 Important Consensus Resolutions: 76.4%

Important Issues		**VOTES**	
1.	IAEA Report	(Y)	Y
2.	U.S. Embargo of Cuba	(N)	Y
3.	National Legislation on Transfer of Arms	(Y)	Y
4.	Nuclear Disarmament	(N)	Y
5.	Risk of Nuclear Proliferation in the Middle East	(N)	Y
6.	Work of the Special Committee to Investigate Israeli Practices	(N)	A
7.	Future Operations of INSTRAW	(N)	Y
8.	Rights of the Child	(N)	Y
9.	Elimination of Racism and Racial Discrimination	(N)	Y
10.	Optional Protocol to the Convention Against Torture	(N)	A
11.	Globalization and Human Rights	(N)	Y
12.	Human Rights in Sudan	(Y)	Y
13.	Human Rights in Iraq	(Y)	Y
14.	Human Rights in the Congo	(Y)	Y

Votes: Y=Yes, N=No, A=Abstain, X=Absent, ( )=U.S. Vote

BAHRAIN

Voting Coincidence Percentages

<u>Overall Votes (90)</u>: Agree 14, Disagree 61, Abstain 9, Absent 6: 18.7%
— Including All 234 Consensus Resolutions: 79.2%
— Arms Control: 20.8%; Human Rights: 17.4%; Middle East: 18.2%

<u>Important Votes (14)</u>: Agree 2, Disagree 10, Abstain 2, Absent 0: 16.7%
— Including the 18 Important Consensus Resolutions: 65.3%

Important Issues	**VOTES**	
1. IAEA Report	(Y)	Y
2. U.S. Embargo of Cuba	(N)	Y
3. National Legislation on Transfer of Arms	(Y)	Y
4. Nuclear Disarmament	(N)	Y
5. Risk of Nuclear Proliferation in the Middle East	(N)	Y
6. Work of the Special Committee to Investigate Israeli Practices	(N)	Y
7. Future Operations of INSTRAW	(N)	Y
8. Rights of the Child	(N)	Y
9. Elimination of Racism and Racial Discrimination	(N)	Y
10. Optional Protocol to the Convention Against Torture	(N)	Y
11. Globalization and Human Rights	(N)	Y
12. Human Rights in Sudan	(Y)	N
13. Human Rights in Iraq	(Y)	A
14. Human Rights in the Congo	(Y)	A

BANGLADESH

Voting Coincidence Percentages

<u>Overall Votes (90)</u>: Agree 16, Disagree 59, Abstain 15, Absent 0: 21.3%
— Including All 234 Consensus Resolutions: 80.9%
— Arms Control: 29.6%; Human Rights: 15.0%; Middle East: 18.2%

<u>Important Votes (14)</u>: Agree 2, Disagree 9, Abstain 3, Absent 0: 18.2%
— Including the 18 Important Consensus Resolutions: 69.0%

Important Issues	**VOTES**	
1. IAEA Report	(Y)	Y
2. U.S. Embargo of Cuba	(N)	Y
3. National Legislation on Transfer of Arms	(Y)	Y
4. Nuclear Disarmament	(N)	Y
5. Risk of Nuclear Proliferation in the Middle East	(N)	Y
6. Work of the Special Committee to Investigate Israeli Practices	(N)	Y
7. Future Operations of INSTRAW	(N)	Y
8. Rights of the Child	(N)	Y
9. Elimination of Racism and Racial Discrimination	(N)	Y
10. Optional Protocol to the Convention Against Torture	(N)	A
11. Globalization and Human Rights	(N)	Y
12. Human Rights in Sudan	(Y)	N
13. Human Rights in Iraq	(Y)	A
14. Human Rights in the Congo	(Y)	A

Votes: Y=Yes, N=No, A=Abstain, X=Absent, ( )=U.S. Vote

BARBADOS

Voting Coincidence Percentages

<u>Overall Votes (90)</u>: Agree 26, Disagree 57, Abstain 4, Absent 3: 31.3%
— Including All 234 Consensus Resolutions: 81.2%
— Arms Control: 35.7%; Human Rights: 40.0%; Middle East: 37.0%

<u>Important Votes (14)</u>: Agree 5, Disagree 8, Abstain 1, Absent 0: 38.5%
— Including the 18 Important Consensus Resolutions: 73.3%

Important Issues		VOTES	
1.	IAEA Report	(Y)	Y
2.	U.S. Embargo of Cuba	(N)	Y
3.	National Legislation on Transfer of Arms	(Y)	Y
4.	Nuclear Disarmament	(N)	Y
5.	Risk of Nuclear Proliferation in the Middle East	(N)	Y
6.	Work of the Special Committee to Investigate Israeli Practices	(N)	A
7.	Future Operations of INSTRAW	(N)	Y
8.	Rights of the Child	(N)	Y
9.	Elimination of Racism and Racial Discrimination	(N)	Y
10.	Optional Protocol to the Convention Against Torture	(N)	Y
11.	Globalization and Human Rights	(N)	Y
12.	Human Rights in Sudan	(Y)	Y
13.	Human Rights in Iraq	(Y)	Y
14.	Human Rights in the Congo	(Y)	Y

BELARUS

Voting Coincidence Percentages

<u>Overall Votes (90)</u>: Agree 14, Disagree 60, Abstain 14, Absent 2: 18.9%
— Including All 234 Consensus Resolutions: 80.2%
— Arms Control: 40.0%; Human Rights: 13.0%; Middle East: 20.8%

<u>Important Votes (14)</u>: Agree 2, Disagree 9, Abstain 3, Absent 0: 18.2%
— Including the 18 Important Consensus Resolutions: 68.6%

Important Issues		VOTES	
1.	IAEA Report	(Y)	Y
2.	U.S. Embargo of Cuba	(N)	Y
3.	National Legislation on Transfer of Arms	(Y)	Y
4.	Nuclear Disarmament	(N)	Y
5.	Risk of Nuclear Proliferation in the Middle East	(N)	Y
6.	Work of the Special Committee to Investigate Israeli Practices	(N)	Y
7.	Future Operations of INSTRAW	(N)	Y
8.	Rights of the Child	(N)	Y
9.	Elimination of Racism and Racial Discrimination	(N)	Y
10.	Optional Protocol to the Convention Against Torture	(N)	Y
11.	Globalization and Human Rights	(N)	Y
12.	Human Rights in Sudan	(Y)	A
13.	Human Rights in Iraq	(Y)	A
14.	Human Rights in the Congo	(Y)	A

Votes: Y=Yes, N=No, A=Abstain, X=Absent, ( )=U.S. Vote

BELGIUM

Voting Coincidence Percentages

<u>Overall Votes (90)</u>: Agree 37, Disagree 37, Abstain 15, Absent 1: 50.0%
— Including All 234 Consensus Resolutions: 87.9%
— Arms Control: 70.8%; Human Rights: 57.1%; Middle East: 45.8%

<u>Important Votes (14)</u>: Agree 6, Disagree 5, Abstain 2, Absent 1: 54.5%
— Including the 18 Important Consensus Resolutions: 82.7%

Important Issues / VOTES

	Issue	U.S.	Vote
1.	IAEA Report	(Y)	Y
2.	U.S. Embargo of Cuba	(N)	Y
3.	National Legislation on Transfer of Arms	(Y)	Y
4.	Nuclear Disarmament	(N)	Y
5.	Risk of Nuclear Proliferation in the Middle East	(N)	X
6.	Work of the Special Committee to Investigate Israeli Practices	(N)	A
7.	Future Operations of INSTRAW	(N)	A
8.	Rights of the Child	(N)	Y
9.	Elimination of Racism and Racial Discrimination	(N)	Y
10.	Optional Protocol to the Convention Against Torture	(N)	Y
11.	Globalization and Human Rights	(N)	N
12.	Human Rights in Sudan	(Y)	Y
13.	Human Rights in Iraq	(Y)	Y
14.	Human Rights in the Congo	(Y)	Y

BELIZE

Voting Coincidence Percentages

<u>Overall Votes (90)</u>: Agree 17, Disagree 58, Abstain 7, Absent 8: 22.7%
— Including All 234 Consensus Resolutions: 79.9%
— Arms Control: 25.0%; Human Rights: 28.0%; Middle East: 10.5%

<u>Important Votes (14)</u>: Agree 4, Disagree 8, Abstain 1, Absent 1: 33.3%
— Including the 18 Important Consensus Resolutions: 71.9%

Important Issues / VOTES

	Issue	U.S.	Vote
1.	IAEA Report	(Y)	X
2.	U.S. Embargo of Cuba	(N)	Y
3.	National Legislation on Transfer of Arms	(Y)	Y
4.	Nuclear Disarmament	(N)	Y
5.	Risk of Nuclear Proliferation in the Middle East	(N)	Y
6.	Work of the Special Committee to Investigate Israeli Practices	(N)	Y
7.	Future Operations of INSTRAW	(N)	Y
8.	Rights of the Child	(N)	Y
9.	Elimination of Racism and Racial Discrimination	(N)	Y
10.	Optional Protocol to the Convention Against Torture	(N)	A
11.	Globalization and Human Rights	(N)	Y
12.	Human Rights in Sudan	(Y)	Y
13.	Human Rights in Iraq	(Y)	Y
14.	Human Rights in the Congo	(Y)	Y

Votes: Y=Yes, N=No, A=Abstain, X=Absent, ( )=U.S. Vote

BENIN

Voting Coincidence Percentages

Overall Votes (90): Agree 6, Disagree 26, Abstain 6, Absent 52: 18.8%
— Including All 234 Consensus Resolutions: 77.6%
— Arms Control: 0.0%; Human Rights: 23.1%; Middle East: 0.0%

Important Votes (14): Agree 0, Disagree 7, Abstain 2, Absent 5: 0.0%
— Including the 18 Important Consensus Resolutions: 48.0%

Important Issues	VOTES	
1. IAEA Report	(Y)	X
2. U.S. Embargo of Cuba	(N)	Y
3. National Legislation on Transfer of Arms	(Y)	X
4. Nuclear Disarmament	(N)	X
5. Risk of Nuclear Proliferation in the Middle East	(N)	X
6. Work of the Special Committee to Investigate Israeli Practices	(N)	X
7. Future Operations of INSTRAW	(N)	Y
8. Rights of the Child	(N)	Y
9. Elimination of Racism and Racial Discrimination	(N)	Y
10. Optional Protocol to the Convention Against Torture	(N)	Y
11. Globalization and Human Rights	(N)	Y
12. Human Rights in Sudan	(Y)	N
13. Human Rights in Iraq	(Y)	A
14. Human Rights in the Congo	(Y)	A

BHUTAN

Voting Coincidence Percentages

Overall Votes (90): Agree 8, Disagree 42, Abstain 15, Absent 25: 16.0%
— Including All 234 Consensus Resolutions: 80.3%
— Arms Control: 22.7%; Human Rights: 16.7%; Middle East: 10.0%

Important Votes (14): Agree 2, Disagree 7, Abstain 3, Absent 2: 22.2%
— Including the 18 Important Consensus Resolutions: 67.5%

Important Issues	VOTES	
1. IAEA Report	(Y)	X
2. U.S. Embargo of Cuba	(N)	Y
3. National Legislation on Transfer of Arms	(Y)	Y
4. Nuclear Disarmament	(N)	Y
5. Risk of Nuclear Proliferation in the Middle East	(N)	Y
6. Work of the Special Committee to Investigate Israeli Practices	(N)	X
7. Future Operations of INSTRAW	(N)	Y
8. Rights of the Child	(N)	Y
9. Elimination of Racism and Racial Discrimination	(N)	Y
10. Optional Protocol to the Convention Against Torture	(N)	A
11. Globalization and Human Rights	(N)	Y
12. Human Rights in Sudan	(Y)	A
13. Human Rights in Iraq	(Y)	Y
14. Human Rights in the Congo	(Y)	A

Votes: Y=Yes, N=No, A=Abstain, X=Absent, ( )=U.S. Vote

BOLIVIA

Voting Coincidence Percentages

<u>Overall Votes (90)</u>: Agree 26, Disagree 63, Abstain 1, Absent 0: 29.2%
— Including All 234 Consensus Resolutions: 80.5%
— Arms Control: 37.9%; Human Rights: 37.5%; Middle East: 37.9%

<u>Important Votes (14)</u>: Agree 5, Disagree 9, Abstain 0, Absent 0: 35.7%
— Including the 18 Important Consensus Resolutions: 71.9%

Important Issues		**VOTES**
1. IAEA Report	(Y)	Y
2. U.S. Embargo of Cuba	(N)	Y
3. National Legislation on Transfer of Arms	(Y)	Y
4. Nuclear Disarmament	(N)	Y
5. Risk of Nuclear Proliferation in the Middle East	(N)	Y
6. Work of the Special Committee to Investigate Israeli Practices	(N)	Y
7. Future Operations of INSTRAW	(N)	Y
8. Rights of the Child	(N)	Y
9. Elimination of Racism and Racial Discrimination	(N)	Y
10. Optional Protocol to the Convention Against Torture	(N)	Y
11. Globalization and Human Rights	(N)	Y
12. Human Rights in Sudan	(Y)	Y
13. Human Rights in Iraq	(Y)	Y
14. Human Rights in the Congo	(Y)	Y

BOSNIA AND HERZEGOVINA

Voting Coincidence Percentages

<u>Overall Votes (90)</u>: Agree 35, Disagree 34, Abstain 14, Absent 7: 50.7%
— Including All 234 Consensus Resolutions: 88.1%
— Arms Control: 69.6%; Human Rights: 58.6%; Middle East: 44.0%

<u>Important Votes (14)</u>: Agree 6, Disagree 6, Abstain 2, Absent 0: 50.0%
— Including the 18 Important Consensus Resolutions: 79.1%

Important Issues		**VOTES**
1. IAEA Report	(Y)	Y
2. U.S. Embargo of Cuba	(N)	Y
3. National Legislation on Transfer of Arms	(Y)	Y
4. Nuclear Disarmament	(N)	Y
5. Risk of Nuclear Proliferation in the Middle East	(N)	Y
6. Work of the Special Committee to Investigate Israeli Practices	(N)	A
7. Future Operations of INSTRAW	(N)	A
8. Rights of the Child	(N)	Y
9. Elimination of Racism and Racial Discrimination	(N)	Y
10. Optional Protocol to the Convention Against Torture	(N)	Y
11. Globalization and Human Rights	(N)	N
12. Human Rights in Sudan	(Y)	Y
13. Human Rights in Iraq	(Y)	Y
14. Human Rights in the Congo	(Y)	Y

Votes: Y=Yes, N=No, A=Abstain, X=Absent, ( )=U.S. Vote

BOTSWANA

Voting Coincidence Percentages

<u>Overall Votes (90)</u>: Agree 11, Disagree 56, Abstain 13, Absent 10: 16.4%
— Including All 234 Consensus Resolutions: 79.3%
— Arms Control: 26.1%; Human Rights: 15.8%; Middle East: 5.6%

<u>Important Votes (14)</u>: Agree 1, Disagree 9, Abstain 3, Absent 1: 10.0%
— Including the 18 Important Consensus Resolutions: 64.9%

Important Issues		VOTES
1. IAEA Report	(Y)	X
2. U.S. Embargo of Cuba	(N)	Y
3. National Legislation on Transfer of Arms	(Y)	Y
4. Nuclear Disarmament	(N)	Y
5. Risk of Nuclear Proliferation in the Middle East	(N)	Y
6. Work of the Special Committee to Investigate Israeli Practices	(N)	Y
7. Future Operations of INSTRAW	(N)	Y
8. Rights of the Child	(N)	Y
9. Elimination of Racism and Racial Discrimination	(N)	Y
10. Optional Protocol to the Convention Against Torture	(N)	Y
11. Globalization and Human Rights	(N)	Y
12. Human Rights in Sudan	(Y)	A
13. Human Rights in Iraq	(Y)	A
14. Human Rights in the Congo	(Y)	A

BRAZIL

Voting Coincidence Percentages

<u>Overall Votes (90)</u>: Agree 26, Disagree 58, Abstain 6, Absent 0: 31.0%
— Including All 234 Consensus Resolutions: 81.8%
— Arms Control: 42.3%; Human Rights: 40.0%; Middle East: 39.3%

<u>Important Votes (14)</u>: Agree 5, Disagree 8, Abstain 1, Absent 0: 38.5%
— Including the 18 Important Consensus Resolutions: 74.2%

Important Issues		VOTES
1. IAEA Report	(Y)	Y
2. U.S. Embargo of Cuba	(N)	Y
3. National Legislation on Transfer of Arms	(Y)	Y
4. Nuclear Disarmament	(N)	A
5. Risk of Nuclear Proliferation in the Middle East	(N)	Y
6. Work of the Special Committee to Investigate Israeli Practices	(N)	Y
7. Future Operations of INSTRAW	(N)	Y
8. Rights of the Child	(N)	Y
9. Elimination of Racism and Racial Discrimination	(N)	Y
10. Optional Protocol to the Convention Against Torture	(N)	Y
11. Globalization and Human Rights	(N)	Y
12. Human Rights in Sudan	(Y)	Y
13. Human Rights in Iraq	(Y)	Y
14. Human Rights in the Congo	(Y)	Y

Votes: Y=Yes, N=No, A=Abstain, X=Absent, ( )=U.S. Vote

BRUNEI DARUSSALAM

Voting Coincidence Percentages

Overall Votes (90): Agree 16, Disagree 59, Abstain 15, Absent 0: 21.3%
— Including All 234 Consensus Resolutions: 80.9%
— Arms Control: 32.1%; Human Rights: 10.5%; Middle East: 21.7%

Important Votes (14): Agree 2, Disagree 9, Abstain 3, Absent 0: 18.2%
— Including the 18 Important Consensus Resolutions: 69.0%

Important Issues

			VOTES	
1.	IAEA Report		(Y)	Y
2.	U.S. Embargo of Cuba		(N)	Y
3.	National Legislation on Transfer of Arms		(Y)	Y
4.	Nuclear Disarmament		(N)	Y
5.	Risk of Nuclear Proliferation in the Middle East		(N)	Y
6.	Work of the Special Committee to Investigate Israeli Practices		(N)	Y
7.	Future Operations of INSTRAW		(N)	Y
8.	Rights of the Child		(N)	Y
9.	Elimination of Racism and Racial Discrimination		(N)	Y
10.	Optional Protocol to the Convention Against Torture		(N)	A
11.	Globalization and Human Rights		(N)	Y
12.	Human Rights in Sudan		(Y)	N
13.	Human Rights in Iraq		(Y)	A
14.	Human Rights in the Congo		(Y)	A

BULGARIA

Voting Coincidence Percentages

Overall Votes (90): Agree 37, Disagree 38, Abstain 14, Absent 1: 49.3%
— Including All 234 Consensus Resolutions: 87.6%
— Arms Control: 69.2%; Human Rights: 58.6%; Middle East: 44.0%

Important Votes (14): Agree 6, Disagree 6, Abstain 2, Absent 0: 50.0%
— Including the 18 Important Consensus Resolutions: 79.9%
Security Council Votes: 100.0%

Important Issues

			VOTES	
1.	IAEA Report		(Y)	Y
2.	U.S. Embargo of Cuba		(N)	Y
3.	National Legislation on Transfer of Arms		(Y)	Y
4.	Nuclear Disarmament		(N)	Y
5.	Risk of Nuclear Proliferation in the Middle East		(N)	Y
6.	Work of the Special Committee to Investigate Israeli Practices		(N)	A
7.	Future Operations of INSTRAW		(N)	A
8.	Rights of the Child		(N)	Y
9.	Elimination of Racism and Racial Discrimination		(N)	Y
10.	Optional Protocol to the Convention Against Torture		(N)	Y
11.	Globalization and Human Rights		(N)	N
12.	Human Rights in Sudan		(Y)	Y
13.	Human Rights in Iraq		(Y)	Y
14.	Human Rights in the Congo		(Y)	Y

Votes: Y=Yes, N=No, A=Abstain, X=Absent, ( )=U.S. Vote

BURKINA FASO

Voting Coincidence Percentages

Overall Votes (90): Agree 16, Disagree 60, Abstain 14, Absent 0: 21.1%
— Including All 234 Consensus Resolutions: 80.5%
— Arms Control: 36.7%; Human Rights: 10.0%; Middle East: 25.0%

Important Votes (14): Agree 2, Disagree 10, Abstain 2, Absent 0: 16.7%
— Including the 18 Important Consensus Resolutions: 66.5%

Important Issues		VOTES
1. IAEA Report	(Y)	Y
2. U.S. Embargo of Cuba	(N)	Y
3. National Legislation on Transfer of Arms	(Y)	Y
4. Nuclear Disarmament	(N)	Y
5. Risk of Nuclear Proliferation in the Middle East	(N)	Y
6. Work of the Special Committee to Investigate Israeli Practices	(N)	Y
7. Future Operations of INSTRAW	(N)	Y
8. Rights of the Child	(N)	Y
9. Elimination of Racism and Racial Discrimination	(N)	Y
10. Optional Protocol to the Convention Against Torture	(N)	Y
11. Globalization and Human Rights	(N)	Y
12. Human Rights in Sudan	(Y)	N
13. Human Rights in Iraq	(Y)	A
14. Human Rights in the Congo	(Y)	A

BURUNDI

Voting Coincidence Percentages

Overall Votes (90): Agree 16, Disagree 46, Abstain 8, Absent 20: 25.8%
— Including All 234 Consensus Resolutions: 81.1%
— Arms Control: 36.7%; Human Rights: 10.0%; Middle East: 35.7%

Important Votes (14): Agree 2, Disagree 9, Abstain 2, Absent 1: 18.2%
— Including the 18 Important Consensus Resolutions: 63.9%

Important Issues		VOTES
1. IAEA Report	(Y)	Y
2. U.S. Embargo of Cuba	(N)	Y
3. National Legislation on Transfer of Arms	(Y)	Y
4. Nuclear Disarmament	(N)	Y
5. Risk of Nuclear Proliferation in the Middle East	(N)	Y
6. Work of the Special Committee to Investigate Israeli Practices	(N)	X
7. Future Operations of INSTRAW	(N)	Y
8. Rights of the Child	(N)	Y
9. Elimination of Racism and Racial Discrimination	(N)	Y
10. Optional Protocol to the Convention Against Torture	(N)	Y
11. Globalization and Human Rights	(N)	Y
12. Human Rights in Sudan	(Y)	N
13. Human Rights in Iraq	(Y)	A
14. Human Rights in the Congo	(Y)	A

Votes: Y=Yes, N=No, A=Abstain, X=Absent, ( )=U.S. Vote

CAMBODIA

Voting Coincidence Percentages

Overall Votes (90): Agree 14, Disagree 58, Abstain 16, Absent 2: 19.4%
— Including All 234 Consensus Resolutions: 80.6%
— Arms Control: 35.7%; Human Rights: 10.5%; Middle East: 21.7%

Important Votes (14): Agree 2, Disagree 10, Abstain 2, Absent 0: 16.7%
— Including the 18 Important Consensus Resolutions: 66.1%

Important Issues

			VOTES
1.	IAEA Report	(Y)	Y
2.	U.S. Embargo of Cuba	(N)	Y
3.	National Legislation on Transfer of Arms	(Y)	Y
4.	Nuclear Disarmament	(N)	Y
5.	Risk of Nuclear Proliferation in the Middle East	(N)	Y
6.	Work of the Special Committee to Investigate Israeli Practices	(N)	Y
7.	Future Operations of INSTRAW	(N)	Y
8.	Rights of the Child	(N)	Y
9.	Elimination of Racism and Racial Discrimination	(N)	Y
10.	Optional Protocol to the Convention Against Torture	(N)	Y
11.	Globalization and Human Rights	(N)	Y
12.	Human Rights in Sudan	(Y)	N
13.	Human Rights in Iraq	(Y)	A
14.	Human Rights in the Congo	(Y)	A

CAMEROON

Voting Coincidence Percentages

Overall Votes (90): Agree 18, Disagree 47, Abstain 13, Absent 12: 27.7%
— Including All 234 Consensus Resolutions: 82.5%
— Arms Control: 35.7%; Human Rights: 22.7%; Middle East: 45.5%

Important Votes (14): Agree 2, Disagree 6, Abstain 5, Absent 1: 25.0%
— Including the 18 Important Consensus Resolutions: 74.6%
Security Council Votes: 98.5%

Important Issues

			VOTES
1.	IAEA Report	(Y)	Y
2.	U.S. Embargo of Cuba	(N)	Y
3.	National Legislation on Transfer of Arms	(Y)	Y
4.	Nuclear Disarmament	(N)	Y
5.	Risk of Nuclear Proliferation in the Middle East	(N)	A
6.	Work of the Special Committee to Investigate Israeli Practices	(N)	X
7.	Future Operations of INSTRAW	(N)	Y
8.	Rights of the Child	(N)	Y
9.	Elimination of Racism and Racial Discrimination	(N)	Y
10.	Optional Protocol to the Convention Against Torture	(N)	A
11.	Globalization and Human Rights	(N)	Y
12.	Human Rights in Sudan	(Y)	A
13.	Human Rights in Iraq	(Y)	A
14.	Human Rights in the Congo	(Y)	A

Votes: Y=Yes, N=No, A=Abstain, X=Absent, ( )=U.S. Vote

CANADA

Voting Coincidence Percentages

Overall Votes (90): Agree 37, Disagree 38, Abstain 15, Absent 0: 49.3%
— Including All 234 Consensus Resolutions: 87.7%
— Arms Control: 64.0%; Human Rights: 61.5%; Middle East: 45.8%

Important Votes (14): Agree 7, Disagree 4, Abstain 3, Absent 0: 63.6%
— Including the 18 Important Consensus Resolutions: 86.2%

Important Issues		VOTES
1. IAEA Report	(Y)	Y
2. U.S. Embargo of Cuba	(N)	Y
3. National Legislation on Transfer of Arms	(Y)	Y
4. Nuclear Disarmament	(N)	Y
5. Risk of Nuclear Proliferation in the Middle East	(N)	A
6. Work of the Special Committee to Investigate Israeli Practices	(N)	A
7. Future Operations of INSTRAW	(N)	N
8. Rights of the Child	(N)	Y
9. Elimination of Racism and Racial Discrimination	(N)	A
10. Optional Protocol to the Convention Against Torture	(N)	Y
11. Globalization and Human Rights	(N)	N
12. Human Rights in Sudan	(Y)	Y
13. Human Rights in Iraq	(Y)	Y
14. Human Rights in the Congo	(Y)	Y

CAPE VERDE

Voting Coincidence Percentages

Overall Votes (90): Agree 14, Disagree 59, Abstain 13, Absent 4: 19.2%
— Including All 234 Consensus Resolutions: 80.2%
— Arms Control: 34.5%; Human Rights: 10.5%; Middle East: 22.7%

Important Votes (14): Agree 2, Disagree 8, Abstain 3, Absent 1: 20.0%
— Including the 18 Important Consensus Resolutions: 70.7%

Important Issues		VOTES
1. IAEA Report	(Y)	Y
2. U.S. Embargo of Cuba	(N)	Y
3. National Legislation on Transfer of Arms	(Y)	Y
4. Nuclear Disarmament	(N)	Y
5. Risk of Nuclear Proliferation in the Middle East	(N)	Y
6. Work of the Special Committee to Investigate Israeli Practices	(N)	X
7. Future Operations of INSTRAW	(N)	Y
8. Rights of the Child	(N)	Y
9. Elimination of Racism and Racial Discrimination	(N)	Y
10. Optional Protocol to the Convention Against Torture	(N)	Y
11. Globalization and Human Rights	(N)	Y
12. Human Rights in Sudan	(Y)	A
13. Human Rights in Iraq	(Y)	A
14. Human Rights in the Congo	(Y)	A

Votes: Y=Yes, N=No, A=Abstain, X=Absent, ( )=U.S. Vote

CENTRAL AFRICAN REPUBLIC

Voting Coincidence Percentages

<u>Overall Votes (90)</u>: Agree 0, Disagree 0, Abstain 0, Absent 90: 0.0%
— Including All 234 Consensus Resolutions: 0.0%
— Arms Control: 0.0%; Human Rights: 0.0%; Middle East: 0.0%

<u>Important Votes (14)</u>: Agree 0, Disagree 0, Abstain 0, Absent 14: 0.0%
— Including the 18 Important Consensus Resolutions: 0.0%

Important Issues

		VOTES	
1.	IAEA Report	(Y)	X
2.	U.S. Embargo of Cuba	(N)	X
3.	National Legislation on Transfer of Arms	(Y)	X
4.	Nuclear Disarmament	(N)	X
5.	Risk of Nuclear Proliferation in the Middle East	(N)	X
6.	Work of the Special Committee to Investigate Israeli Practices	(N)	X
7.	Future Operations of INSTRAW	(N)	X
8.	Rights of the Child	(N)	X
9.	Elimination of Racism and Racial Discrimination	(N)	X
10.	Optional Protocol to the Convention Against Torture	(N)	X
11.	Globalization and Human Rights	(N)	X
12.	Human Rights in Sudan	(Y)	X
13.	Human Rights in Iraq	(Y)	X
14.	Human Rights in the Congo	(Y)	X

CHAD

Voting Coincidence Percentages

<u>Overall Votes (90)</u>: Agree 3, Disagree 28, Abstain 10, Absent 49: 9.7%
— Including All 234 Consensus Resolutions: 78.5%
— Arms Control: 0.0%; Human Rights: 12.5%; Middle East: 11.1%

<u>Important Votes (14)</u>: Agree 0, Disagree 4, Abstain 2, Absent 8: 0.0%
— Including the 18 Important Consensus Resolutions: 65.6%

Important Issues

		VOTES	
1.	IAEA Report	(Y)	X
2.	U.S. Embargo of Cuba	(N)	Y
3.	National Legislation on Transfer of Arms	(Y)	X
4.	Nuclear Disarmament	(N)	X
5.	Risk of Nuclear Proliferation in the Middle East	(N)	X
6.	Work of the Special Committee to Investigate Israeli Practices	(N)	Y
7.	Future Operations of INSTRAW	(N)	X
8.	Rights of the Child	(N)	X
9.	Elimination of Racism and Racial Discrimination	(N)	X
10.	Optional Protocol to the Convention Against Torture	(N)	X
11.	Globalization and Human Rights	(N)	Y
12.	Human Rights in Sudan	(Y)	N
13.	Human Rights in Iraq	(Y)	A
14.	Human Rights in the Congo	(Y)	A

Votes: Y=Yes, N=No, A=Abstain, X=Absent, ( )=U.S. Vote

CHILE

Voting Coincidence Percentages

<u>Overall Votes (90):</u> Agree 27, Disagree 61, Abstain 2, Absent 0: 30.7%
— Including All 234 Consensus Resolutions: 81.1%
— Arms Control: 37.9%; Human Rights: 43.3%; Middle East: 37.9%

<u>Important Votes (14):</u> Agree 5, Disagree 9, Abstain 0, Absent 0: 35.7%
— Including the 18 Important Consensus Resolutions: 71.9%

Important Issues		VOTES
1.	IAEA Report	(Y) Y
2.	U.S. Embargo of Cuba	(N) Y
3.	National Legislation on Transfer of Arms	(Y) Y
4.	Nuclear Disarmament	(N) Y
5.	Risk of Nuclear Proliferation in the Middle East	(N) Y
6.	Work of the Special Committee to Investigate Israeli Practices	(N) Y
7.	Future Operations of INSTRAW	(N) Y
8.	Rights of the Child	(N) Y
9.	Elimination of Racism and Racial Discrimination	(N) Y
10.	Optional Protocol to the Convention Against Torture	(N) Y
11.	Globalization and Human Rights	(N) Y
12.	Human Rights in Sudan	(Y) Y
13.	Human Rights in Iraq	(Y) Y
14.	Human Rights in the Congo	(Y) Y

CHINA

Voting Coincidence Percentages

<u>Overall Votes (90):</u> Agree 13, Disagree 61, Abstain 13, Absent 3: 17.6%
— Including All 234 Consensus Resolutions: 79.8%
— Arms Control: 27.3%; Human Rights: 15.4%; Middle East: 18.5%

<u>Important Votes (14):</u> Agree 2, Disagree 8, Abstain 4, Absent 0: 20.0%
— Including the 18 Important Consensus Resolutions: 70.9%
Security Council Votes: 97.1%

Important Issues		VOTES
1.	IAEA Report	(Y) Y
2.	U.S. Embargo of Cuba	(N) Y
3.	National Legislation on Transfer of Arms	(Y) Y
4.	Nuclear Disarmament	(N) A
5.	Risk of Nuclear Proliferation in the Middle East	(N) Y
6.	Work of the Special Committee to Investigate Israeli Practices	(N) Y
7.	Future Operations of INSTRAW	(N) Y
8.	Rights of the Child	(N) Y
9.	Elimination of Racism and Racial Discrimination	(N) Y
10.	Optional Protocol to the Convention Against Torture	(N) A
11.	Globalization and Human Rights	(N) Y
12.	Human Rights in Sudan	(Y) N
13.	Human Rights in Iraq	(Y) A
14.	Human Rights in the Congo	(Y) A

Votes: Y=Yes, N=No, A=Abstain, X=Absent, ( )=U.S. Vote

COLOMBIA

Voting Coincidence Percentages

<u>Overall Votes (90)</u>: Agree 24, Disagree 60, Abstain 3, Absent 3: 28.6%
— Including All 234 Consensus Resolutions: 80.7%
— Arms Control: 39.3%; Human Rights: 36.7%; Middle East: 37.9%

<u>Important Votes (14)</u>: Agree 5, Disagree 8, Abstain 1, Absent 0: 38.5%
— Including the 18 Important Consensus Resolutions: 73.8%
Security Council Votes: 97.1%

Important Issues	VOTES	
1. IAEA Report	(Y)	Y
2. U.S. Embargo of Cuba	(N)	Y
3. National Legislation on Transfer of Arms	(Y)	Y
4. Nuclear Disarmament	(N)	Y
5. Risk of Nuclear Proliferation in the Middle East	(N)	Y
6. Work of the Special Committee to Investigate Israeli Practices	(N)	Y
7. Future Operations of INSTRAW	(N)	Y
8. Rights of the Child	(N)	Y
9. Elimination of Racism and Racial Discrimination	(N)	Y
10. Optional Protocol to the Convention Against Torture	(N)	Y
11. Globalization and Human Rights	(N)	A
12. Human Rights in Sudan	(Y)	Y
13. Human Rights in Iraq	(Y)	Y
14. Human Rights in the Congo	(Y)	Y

COMOROS

Voting Coincidence Percentages

<u>Overall Votes (90)</u>: Agree 9, Disagree 47, Abstain 11, Absent 23: 16.1%
— Including All 234 Consensus Resolutions: 79.2%
— Arms Control: 15.0%; Human Rights: 17.4%; Middle East: 0.0%

<u>Important Votes (14)</u>: Agree 1, Disagree 8, Abstain 2, Absent 3: 11.1%
— Including the 18 Important Consensus Resolutions: 63.8%

Important Issues	VOTES	
1. IAEA Report	(Y)	X
2. U.S. Embargo of Cuba	(N)	Y
3. National Legislation on Transfer of Arms	(Y)	Y
4. Nuclear Disarmament	(N)	Y
5. Risk of Nuclear Proliferation in the Middle East	(N)	Y
6. Work of the Special Committee to Investigate Israeli Practices	(N)	X
7. Future Operations of INSTRAW	(N)	Y
8. Rights of the Child	(N)	Y
9. Elimination of Racism and Racial Discrimination	(N)	Y
10. Optional Protocol to the Convention Against Torture	(N)	X
11. Globalization and Human Rights	(N)	Y
12. Human Rights in Sudan	(Y)	N
13. Human Rights in Iraq	(Y)	A
14. Human Rights in the Congo	(Y)	A

Votes: Y=Yes, N=No, A=Abstain, X=Absent, ( )=U.S. Vote

CONGO

Voting Coincidence Percentages

Overall Votes (90): Agree 14, Disagree 61, Abstain 6, Absent 9: 18.7%
— Including All 234 Consensus Resolutions: 78.2%
— Arms Control: 32.0%; Human Rights: 19.2%; Middle East: 14.3%

Important Votes (14): Agree 2, Disagree 10, Abstain 2, Absent 0: 16.7%
— Including the 18 Important Consensus Resolutions: 64.0%

Important Issues	**VOTES**	
1. IAEA Report	(Y)	Y
2. U.S. Embargo of Cuba	(N)	Y
3. National Legislation on Transfer of Arms	(Y)	Y
4. Nuclear Disarmament	(N)	Y
5. Risk of Nuclear Proliferation in the Middle East	(N)	Y
6. Work of the Special Committee to Investigate Israeli Practices	(N)	Y
7. Future Operations of INSTRAW	(N)	Y
8. Rights of the Child	(N)	Y
9. Elimination of Racism and Racial Discrimination	(N)	Y
10. Optional Protocol to the Convention Against Torture	(N)	Y
11. Globalization and Human Rights	(N)	Y
12. Human Rights in Sudan	(Y)	N
13. Human Rights in Iraq	(Y)	A
14. Human Rights in the Congo	(Y)	A

COSTA RICA

Voting Coincidence Percentages

Overall Votes (90): Agree 26, Disagree 58, Abstain 3, Absent 3: 31.0%
— Including All 234 Consensus Resolutions: 81.2%
— Arms Control: 37.9%; Human Rights: 36.7%; Middle East: 46.2%

Important Votes (14): Agree 5, Disagree 8, Abstain 1, Absent 0: 38.5%
— Including the 18 Important Consensus Resolutions: 73.6%

Important Issues	**VOTES**	
1. IAEA Report	(Y)	Y
2. U.S. Embargo of Cuba	(N)	Y
3. National Legislation on Transfer of Arms	(Y)	Y
4. Nuclear Disarmament	(N)	Y
5. Risk of Nuclear Proliferation in the Middle East	(N)	Y
6. Work of the Special Committee to Investigate Israeli Practices	(N)	A
7. Future Operations of INSTRAW	(N)	Y
8. Rights of the Child	(N)	Y
9. Elimination of Racism and Racial Discrimination	(N)	Y
10. Optional Protocol to the Convention Against Torture	(N)	Y
11. Globalization and Human Rights	(N)	Y
12. Human Rights in Sudan	(Y)	Y
13. Human Rights in Iraq	(Y)	Y
14. Human Rights in the Congo	(Y)	Y

Votes: Y=Yes, N=No, A=Abstain, X=Absent, ( )=U.S. Vote

COTE D'IVOIRE

Voting Coincidence Percentages

Overall Votes (90): Agree 11, Disagree 56, Abstain 7, Absent 16: 16.4%
— Including All 234 Consensus Resolutions: 78.4%
— Arms Control: 22.7%; Human Rights: 21.7%; Middle East: 5.6%

Important Votes (14): Agree 1, Disagree 9, Abstain 2, Absent 2: 10.0%
— Including the 18 Important Consensus Resolutions: 63.7%

Important Issues
VOTES

1.	IAEA Report	(Y)	X
2.	U.S. Embargo of Cuba	(N)	X
3.	National Legislation on Transfer of Arms	(Y)	Y
4.	Nuclear Disarmament	(N)	Y
5.	Risk of Nuclear Proliferation in the Middle East	(N)	Y
6.	Work of the Special Committee to Investigate Israeli Practices	(N)	Y
7.	Future Operations of INSTRAW	(N)	Y
8.	Rights of the Child	(N)	Y
9.	Elimination of Racism and Racial Discrimination	(N)	Y
10.	Optional Protocol to the Convention Against Torture	(N)	Y
11.	Globalization and Human Rights	(N)	Y
12.	Human Rights in Sudan	(Y)	N
13.	Human Rights in Iraq	(Y)	A
14.	Human Rights in the Congo	(Y)	A

CROATIA

Voting Coincidence Percentages

Overall Votes (90): Agree 35, Disagree 40, Abstain 15, Absent 0: 46.7%
— Including All 234 Consensus Resolutions: 87.1%
— Arms Control: 66.7%; Human Rights: 55.2%; Middle East: 44.0%

Important Votes (14): Agree 6, Disagree 6, Abstain 2, Absent 0: 50.0%
— Including the 18 Important Consensus Resolutions: 80.0%

Important Issues
VOTES

1.	IAEA Report	(Y)	Y
2.	U.S. Embargo of Cuba	(N)	Y
3.	National Legislation on Transfer of Arms	(Y)	Y
4.	Nuclear Disarmament	(N)	Y
5.	Risk of Nuclear Proliferation in the Middle East	(N)	Y
6.	Work of the Special Committee to Investigate Israeli Practices	(N)	A
7.	Future Operations of INSTRAW	(N)	A
8.	Rights of the Child	(N)	Y
9.	Elimination of Racism and Racial Discrimination	(N)	Y
10.	Optional Protocol to the Convention Against Torture	(N)	Y
11.	Globalization and Human Rights	(N)	N
12.	Human Rights in Sudan	(Y)	Y
13.	Human Rights in Iraq	(Y)	Y
14.	Human Rights in the Congo	(Y)	Y

Votes: Y=Yes, N=No, A=Abstain, X=Absent, ( )=U.S. Vote

CUBA

Voting Coincidence Percentages

Overall Votes (90): Agree 12, Disagree 62, Abstain 8, Absent 8: 16.2%
— Including All 234 Consensus Resolutions: 78.5%
— Arms Control: 24.0%; Human Rights: 9.1%; Middle East: 14.8%

Important Votes (14): Agree 2, Disagree 8, Abstain 4, Absent 0: 20.0%
— Including the 18 Important Consensus Resolutions: 69.8%

Important Issues		VOTES
1. IAEA Report	(Y)	Y
2. U.S. Embargo of Cuba	(N)	Y
3. National Legislation on Transfer of Arms	(Y)	Y
4. Nuclear Disarmament	(N)	A
5. Risk of Nuclear Proliferation in the Middle East	(N)	Y
6. Work of the Special Committee to Investigate Israeli Practices	(N)	Y
7. Future Operations of INSTRAW	(N)	Y
8. Rights of the Child	(N)	Y
9. Elimination of Racism and Racial Discrimination	(N)	Y
10. Optional Protocol to the Convention Against Torture	(N)	A
11. Globalization and Human Rights	(N)	Y
12. Human Rights in Sudan	(Y)	N
13. Human Rights in Iraq	(Y)	A
14. Human Rights in the Congo	(Y)	A

CYPRUS

Voting Coincidence Percentages

Overall Votes (90): Agree 34, Disagree 49, Abstain 7, Absent 0: 41.0%
— Including All 234 Consensus Resolutions: 84.5%
— Arms Control: 57.7%; Human Rights: 56.7%; Middle East: 37.9%

Important Votes (14): Agree 6, Disagree 8, Abstain 0, Absent 0: 42.9%
— Including the 18 Important Consensus Resolutions: 75.0%

Important Issues		VOTES
1. IAEA Report	(Y)	Y
2. U.S. Embargo of Cuba	(N)	Y
3. National Legislation on Transfer of Arms	(Y)	Y
4. Nuclear Disarmament	(N)	Y
5. Risk of Nuclear Proliferation in the Middle East	(N)	Y
6. Work of the Special Committee to Investigate Israeli Practices	(N)	Y
7. Future Operations of INSTRAW	(N)	Y
8. Rights of the Child	(N)	Y
9. Elimination of Racism and Racial Discrimination	(N)	Y
10. Optional Protocol to the Convention Against Torture	(N)	Y
11. Globalization and Human Rights	(N)	N
12. Human Rights in Sudan	(Y)	Y
13. Human Rights in Iraq	(Y)	Y
14. Human Rights in the Congo	(Y)	Y

Votes: Y=Yes, N=No, A=Abstain, X=Absent, ( )=U.S. Vote

CZECH REPUBLIC

Voting Coincidence Percentages

Overall Votes (90): Agree 37, Disagree 40, Abstain 12, Absent 1: 48.1%
— Including All 234 Consensus Resolutions: 87.0%
— Arms Control: 68.0%; Human Rights: 58.6%; Middle East: 44.0%

Important Votes (14): Agree 6, Disagree 7, Abstain 1, Absent 0: 46.2%
— Including the 18 Important Consensus Resolutions: 77.3%

Important Issues   VOTES

1.	IAEA Report	(Y)	Y
2.	U.S. Embargo of Cuba	(N)	Y
3.	National Legislation on Transfer of Arms	(Y)	Y
4.	Nuclear Disarmament	(N)	Y
5.	Risk of Nuclear Proliferation in the Middle East	(N)	Y
6.	Work of the Special Committee to Investigate Israeli Practices	(N)	A
7.	Future Operations of INSTRAW	(N)	Y
8.	Rights of the Child	(N)	Y
9.	Elimination of Racism and Racial Discrimination	(N)	Y
10.	Optional Protocol to the Convention Against Torture	(N)	Y
11.	Globalization and Human Rights	(N)	N
12.	Human Rights in Sudan	(Y)	Y
13.	Human Rights in Iraq	(Y)	Y
14.	Human Rights in the Congo	(Y)	Y

DEMOCRATIC PEOPLE'S REPUBLIC OF KOREA

Voting Coincidence Percentages

Overall Votes (90): Agree 7, Disagree 57, Abstain 11, Absent 15: 10.9%
— Including All 234 Consensus Resolutions: 77.5%
— Arms Control: 0.0%; Human Rights: 14.3%; Middle East: 5.0%

Important Votes (14): Agree 0, Disagree 9, Abstain 3, Absent 2: 0.0%
— Including the 18 Important Consensus Resolutions: 61.9%

Important Issues   VOTES

1.	IAEA Report	(Y)	N
2.	U.S. Embargo of Cuba	(N)	Y
3.	National Legislation on Transfer of Arms	(Y)	X
4.	Nuclear Disarmament	(N)	A
5.	Risk of Nuclear Proliferation in the Middle East	(N)	Y
6.	Work of the Special Committee to Investigate Israeli Practices	(N)	Y
7.	Future Operations of INSTRAW	(N)	Y
8.	Rights of the Child	(N)	Y
9.	Elimination of Racism and Racial Discrimination	(N)	Y
10.	Optional Protocol to the Convention Against Torture	(N)	X
11.	Globalization and Human Rights	(N)	Y
12.	Human Rights in Sudan	(Y)	N
13.	Human Rights in Iraq	(Y)	A
14.	Human Rights in the Congo	(Y)	A

Votes: Y=Yes, N=No, A=Abstain, X=Absent, ( )=U.S. Vote

DEMOCRATIC REPUBLIC OF THE CONGO

Voting Coincidence Percentages

Overall Votes (90): Agree 2, Disagree 34, Abstain 13, Absent 41: 5.6%
— Including All 234 Consensus Resolutions: 77.8%
— Arms Control: 0.0%; Human Rights: 5.3%; Middle East: 0.0%

Important Votes (14): Agree 0, Disagree 7, Abstain 2, Absent 5: 0.0%
— Including the 18 Important Consensus Resolutions: 56.3%

Important Issues		VOTES
1.	IAEA Report	(Y) X
2.	U.S. Embargo of Cuba	(N) Y
3.	National Legislation on Transfer of Arms	(Y) X
4.	Nuclear Disarmament	(N) X
5.	Risk of Nuclear Proliferation in the Middle East	(N) X
6.	Work of the Special Committee to Investigate Israeli Practices	(N) X
7.	Future Operations of INSTRAW	(N) Y
8.	Rights of the Child	(N) Y
9.	Elimination of Racism and Racial Discrimination	(N) Y
10.	Optional Protocol to the Convention Against Torture	(N) Y
11.	Globalization and Human Rights	(Y) N
12.	Human Rights in Sudan	(Y) N
13.	Human Rights in Iraq	(Y) A
14.	Human Rights in the Congo	(Y) A

DENMARK

Voting Coincidence Percentages

Overall Votes (90): Agree 37, Disagree 39, Abstain 13, Absent 1: 48.7%
— Including All 234 Consensus Resolutions: 87.3%
— Arms Control: 68.0%; Human Rights: 57.1%; Middle East: 44.0%

Important Votes (14): Agree 6, Disagree 6, Abstain 2, Absent 0: 50.0%
— Including the 18 Important Consensus Resolutions: 79.9%

Important Issues		VOTES
1.	IAEA Report	(Y) Y
2.	U.S. Embargo of Cuba	(N) Y
3.	National Legislation on Transfer of Arms	(Y) Y
4.	Nuclear Disarmament	(N) Y
5.	Risk of Nuclear Proliferation in the Middle East	(N) Y
6.	Work of the Special Committee to Investigate Israeli Practices	(N) A
7.	Future Operations of INSTRAW	(N) A
8.	Rights of the Child	(N) Y
9.	Elimination of Racism and Racial Discrimination	(N) Y
10.	Optional Protocol to the Convention Against Torture	(N) Y
11.	Globalization and Human Rights	(N) N
12.	Human Rights in Sudan	(Y) Y
13.	Human Rights in Iraq	(Y) Y
14.	Human Rights in the Congo	(Y) Y

Votes: Y=Yes, N=No, A=Abstain, X=Absent, ( )=U.S. Vote

DJIBOUTI

Voting Coincidence Percentages

Overall Votes (90): Agree 16, Disagree 62, Abstain 9, Absent 3: 20.5%
— Including All 234 Consensus Resolutions: 79.7%
— Arms Control: 29.6%; Human Rights: 13.0%; Middle East: 21.7%

Important Votes (14): Agree 2, Disagree 9, Abstain 3, Absent 0: 18.2%
— Including the 18 Important Consensus Resolutions: 68.4%

Important Issues

		VOTES	
1.	IAEA Report	(Y)	Y
2.	U.S. Embargo of Cuba	(N)	Y
3.	National Legislation on Transfer of Arms	(Y)	Y
4.	Nuclear Disarmament	(N)	Y
5.	Risk of Nuclear Proliferation in the Middle East	(N)	Y
6.	Work of the Special Committee to Investigate Israeli Practices	(N)	Y
7.	Future Operations of INSTRAW	(N)	Y
8.	Rights of the Child	(N)	Y
9.	Elimination of Racism and Racial Discrimination	(N)	Y
10.	Optional Protocol to the Convention Against Torture	(N)	A
11.	Globalization and Human Rights	(N)	Y
12.	Human Rights in Sudan	(Y)	N
13.	Human Rights in Iraq	(Y)	A
14.	Human Rights in the Congo	(Y)	A

DOMINICA

Voting Coincidence Percentages

Overall Votes (90): Agree 13, Disagree 32, Abstain 9, Absent 36: 28.9%
— Including All 234 Consensus Resolutions: 81.7%
— Arms Control: 28.6%; Human Rights: 21.7%; Middle East: 0.0%

Important Votes (14): Agree 0, Disagree 8, Abstain 3, Absent 3: 0.0%
— Including the 18 Important Consensus Resolutions: 55.6%

Important Issues

		VOTES	
1.	IAEA Report	(Y)	X
2.	U.S. Embargo of Cuba	(N)	Y
3.	National Legislation on Transfer of Arms	(Y)	X
4.	Nuclear Disarmament	(N)	Y
5.	Risk of Nuclear Proliferation in the Middle East	(N)	Y
6.	Work of the Special Committee to Investigate Israeli Practices	(N)	X
7.	Future Operations of INSTRAW	(N)	Y
8.	Rights of the Child	(N)	Y
9.	Elimination of Racism and Racial Discrimination	(N)	Y
10.	Optional Protocol to the Convention Against Torture	(N)	Y
11.	Globalization and Human Rights	(N)	Y
12.	Human Rights in Sudan	(Y)	A
13.	Human Rights in Iraq	(Y)	A
14.	Human Rights in the Congo	(Y)	A

Votes: Y=Yes, N=No, A=Abstain, X=Absent, ( )=U.S. Vote

DOMINICAN REPUBLIC

Voting Coincidence Percentages

Overall Votes (90): Agree 26, Disagree 64, Abstain 0, Absent 0: 28.9%
— Including All 234 Consensus Resolutions: 80.2%
— Arms Control: 36.7%; Human Rights: 37.5%; Middle East: 37.9%

Important Votes (14): Agree 5, Disagree 9, Abstain 0, Absent 0: 35.7%
— Including the 18 Important Consensus Resolutions: 71.9%

Important Issues	VOTES	
1. IAEA Report	(Y)	Y
2. U.S. Embargo of Cuba	(N)	Y
3. National Legislation on Transfer of Arms	(Y)	Y
4. Nuclear Disarmament	(N)	Y
5. Risk of Nuclear Proliferation in the Middle East	(N)	Y
6. Work of the Special Committee to Investigate Israeli Practices	(N)	Y
7. Future Operations of INSTRAW	(N)	Y
8. Rights of the Child	(N)	Y
9. Elimination of Racism and Racial Discrimination	(N)	Y
10. Optional Protocol to the Convention Against Torture	(N)	Y
11. Globalization and Human Rights	(N)	Y
12. Human Rights in Sudan	(Y)	Y
13. Human Rights in Iraq	(Y)	Y
14. Human Rights in the Congo	(Y)	Y

ECUADOR

Voting Coincidence Percentages

Overall Votes (90): Agree 26, Disagree 63, Abstain 1, Absent 0: 29.2%
— Including All 234 Consensus Resolutions: 80.5%
— Arms Control: 36.7%; Human Rights: 38.7%; Middle East: 37.9%

Important Votes (14): Agree 5, Disagree 9, Abstain 0, Absent 0: 35.7%
— Including the 18 Important Consensus Resolutions: 71.9%

Important Issues	VOTES	
1. IAEA Report	(Y)	Y
2. U.S. Embargo of Cuba	(N)	Y
3. National Legislation on Transfer of Arms	(Y)	Y
4. Nuclear Disarmament	(N)	Y
5. Risk of Nuclear Proliferation in the Middle East	(N)	Y
6. Work of the Special Committee to Investigate Israeli Practices	(N)	Y
7. Future Operations of INSTRAW	(N)	Y
8. Rights of the Child	(N)	Y
9. Elimination of Racism and Racial Discrimination	(N)	Y
10. Optional Protocol to the Convention Against Torture	(N)	Y
11. Globalization and Human Rights	(N)	Y
12. Human Rights in Sudan	(Y)	Y
13. Human Rights in Iraq	(Y)	Y
14. Human Rights in the Congo	(Y)	Y

Votes: Y=Yes, N=No, A=Abstain, X=Absent, ( )=U.S. Vote

EGYPT

Voting Coincidence Percentages

<u>Overall Votes (90)</u>: Agree 15, Disagree 60, Abstain 15, Absent 0: 20.0%
— Including All 234 Consensus Resolutions: 80.6%
— Arms Control: 24.0%; Human Rights: 18.2%; Middle East: 21.7%

<u>Important Votes (14)</u>: Agree 2, Disagree 8, Abstain 4, Absent 0: 20.0%
— Including the 18 Important Consensus Resolutions: 71.4%

Important Issues	**VOTES**	
1. IAEA Report	(Y)	Y
2. U.S. Embargo of Cuba	(N)	Y
3. National Legislation on Transfer of Arms	(Y)	Y
4. Nuclear Disarmament	(N)	A
5. Risk of Nuclear Proliferation in the Middle East	(N)	Y
6. Work of the Special Committee to Investigate Israeli Practices	(N)	Y
7. Future Operations of INSTRAW	(N)	Y
8. Rights of the Child	(N)	Y
9. Elimination of Racism and Racial Discrimination	(N)	Y
10. Optional Protocol to the Convention Against Torture	(N)	A
11. Globalization and Human Rights	(N)	Y
12. Human Rights in Sudan	(Y)	N
13. Human Rights in Iraq	(Y)	A
14. Human Rights in the Congo	(Y)	A

EL SALVADOR

Voting Coincidence Percentages

<u>Overall Votes (90)</u>: Agree 26, Disagree 54, Abstain 2, Absent 8: 32.5%
— Including All 234 Consensus Resolutions: 81.6%
— Arms Control: 37.9%; Human Rights: 38.7%; Middle East: 44.0%

<u>Important Votes (14)</u>: Agree 5, Disagree 6, Abstain 0, Absent 3: 45.5%
— Including the 18 Important Consensus Resolutions: 78.2%

Important Issues	**VOTES**	
1. IAEA Report	(Y)	Y
2. U.S. Embargo of Cuba	(N)	X
3. National Legislation on Transfer of Arms	(Y)	Y
4. Nuclear Disarmament	(N)	Y
5. Risk of Nuclear Proliferation in the Middle East	(N)	Y
6. Work of the Special Committee to Investigate Israeli Practices	(N)	X
7. Future Operations of INSTRAW	(N)	X
8. Rights of the Child	(N)	Y
9. Elimination of Racism and Racial Discrimination	(N)	Y
10. Optional Protocol to the Convention Against Torture	(N)	Y
11. Globalization and Human Rights	(N)	Y
12. Human Rights in Sudan	(Y)	Y
13. Human Rights in Iraq	(Y)	Y
14. Human Rights in the Congo	(Y)	Y

Votes: Y=Yes, N=No, A=Abstain, X=Absent, ( )=U.S. Vote

EQUATORIAL GUINEA

Voting Coincidence Percentages

Overall Votes (90): Agree 2, Disagree 21, Abstain 2, Absent 65: 8.7%
— Including All 234 Consensus Resolutions: 73.1%
— Arms Control: 0.0%; Human Rights: 10.5%; Middle East: 0.0%

Important Votes (14): Agree 0, Disagree 7, Abstain 2, Absent 5: 0.0%
— Including the 18 Important Consensus Resolutions: 37.8%

Important Issues		VOTES
1.	IAEA Report	(Y) X
2.	U.S. Embargo of Cuba	(N) Y
3.	National Legislation on Transfer of Arms	(Y) X
4.	Nuclear Disarmament	(N) X
5.	Risk of Nuclear Proliferation in the Middle East	(N) X
6.	Work of the Special Committee to Investigate Israeli Practices	(N) X
7.	Future Operations of INSTRAW	(N) Y
8.	Rights of the Child	(N) Y
9.	Elimination of Racism and Racial Discrimination	(N) Y
10.	Optional Protocol to the Convention Against Torture	(N) Y
11.	Globalization and Human Rights	(N) Y
12.	Human Rights in Sudan	(Y) N
13.	Human Rights in Iraq	(Y) A
14.	Human Rights in the Congo	(Y) A

ERITREA

Voting Coincidence Percentages

Overall Votes (90): Agree 18, Disagree 60, Abstain 9, Absent 3: 23.1%
— Including All 234 Consensus Resolutions: 79.9%
— Arms Control: 34.5%; Human Rights: 21.7%; Middle East: 21.7%

Important Votes (14): Agree 2, Disagree 9, Abstain 3, Absent 0: 18.2%
— Including the 18 Important Consensus Resolutions: 67.8%

Important Issues		VOTES
1.	IAEA Report	(Y) Y
2.	U.S. Embargo of Cuba	(N) Y
3.	National Legislation on Transfer of Arms	(Y) Y
4.	Nuclear Disarmament	(N) Y
5.	Risk of Nuclear Proliferation in the Middle East	(N) Y
6.	Work of the Special Committee to Investigate Israeli Practices	(N) Y
7.	Future Operations of INSTRAW	(N) Y
8.	Rights of the Child	(N) Y
9.	Elimination of Racism and Racial Discrimination	(N) Y
10.	Optional Protocol to the Convention Against Torture	(N) Y
11.	Globalization and Human Rights	(N) Y
12.	Human Rights in Sudan	(Y) A
13.	Human Rights in Iraq	(Y) A
14.	Human Rights in the Congo	(Y) A

Votes: Y=Yes, N=No, A=Abstain, X=Absent, ( )=U.S. Vote

ESTONIA

Voting Coincidence Percentages

Overall Votes (90): Agree 36, Disagree 39, Abstain 14, Absent 1: 48.0%
— Including All 234 Consensus Resolutions: 87.3%
— Arms Control: 66.7%; Human Rights: 57.1%; Middle East: 44.0%

Important Votes (14): Agree 6, Disagree 6, Abstain 2, Absent 0: 50.0%
— Including the 18 Important Consensus Resolutions: 79.9%

Important Issues		**VOTES**
1. IAEA Report	(Y)	Y
2. U.S. Embargo of Cuba	(N)	Y
3. National Legislation on Transfer of Arms	(Y)	Y
4. Nuclear Disarmament	(N)	Y
5. Risk of Nuclear Proliferation in the Middle East	(N)	Y
6. Work of the Special Committee to Investigate Israeli Practices	(N)	A
7. Future Operations of INSTRAW	(N)	A
8. Rights of the Child	(N)	Y
9. Elimination of Racism and Racial Discrimination	(N)	Y
10. Optional Protocol to the Convention Against Torture	(N)	Y
11. Globalization and Human Rights	(N)	N
12. Human Rights in Sudan	(Y)	Y
13. Human Rights in Iraq	(Y)	Y
14. Human Rights in the Congo	(Y)	Y

ETHIOPIA

Voting Coincidence Percentages

Overall Votes (90): Agree 13, Disagree 53, Abstain 18, Absent 6: 19.7%
— Including All 234 Consensus Resolutions: 81.5%
— Arms Control: 30.4%; Human Rights: 5.9%; Middle East: 11.8%

Important Votes (14): Agree 1, Disagree 6, Abstain 6, Absent 1: 14.3%
— Including the 18 Important Consensus Resolutions: 75.0%

Important Issues		**VOTES**
1. IAEA Report	(Y)	X
2. U.S. Embargo of Cuba	(N)	A
3. National Legislation on Transfer of Arms	(Y)	Y
4. Nuclear Disarmament	(N)	Y
5. Risk of Nuclear Proliferation in the Middle East	(N)	A
6. Work of the Special Committee to Investigate Israeli Practices	(N)	A
7. Future Operations of INSTRAW	(N)	Y
8. Rights of the Child	(N)	Y
9. Elimination of Racism and Racial Discrimination	(N)	Y
10. Optional Protocol to the Convention Against Torture	(N)	A
11. Globalization and Human Rights	(N)	Y
12. Human Rights in Sudan	(Y)	N
13. Human Rights in Iraq	(Y)	A
14. Human Rights in the Congo	(Y)	A

Votes: Y=Yes, N=No, A=Abstain, X=Absent, ( )=U.S. Vote

www.ingramcontent.com/pod-product-compliance
Lightning Source LLC
Chambersburg PA
CBHW080756290526
45790CB00008B/3466